How to make a Simple Pot Still

Noel Downs

How to make a Simple Pot Still
Noel Downs
ISBN 978-1481051262
Copyright by Noel Downs 2012.
First Edition published 2012.
First Revised Edition published 2012 by Noel Downs.
All rights reserved under International Copyright Law.
No part of this book may be stored or reproduced in any form
without the express written permission of the publisher.

There are so many people to thank who made this possible. Too many that I would be terrified of leaving someone out. So my thanks to everyone who helped, you know who you are. Many thanks to my teacher Wolfy, and his wife Ilse. Thank you Christine, without you my life would not be possible.

Index

Introduction	5
Distillation Basics	6
Still Types	7
Parts of a Still	8
Parts List	9
Getting started	16
Hints and Tips	16
Compression fittings	16
How they work	17
Steps One to Fourteen	18
Safety Tips	34

Introduction

Distilling of alcohol and essential oils is something humans have done for centuries. If it wasn't for folk like us (and I am including you in this because if the thought had not entered your mind to try your hand at distillation you wouldn't be looking at this book) who like to experiment for our own fun and pleasure to see what is possible, life would be pretty boring. Any way before we go any further, this book is not about how to distill, there are plenty of books and information on the web about the fine art, this book is a simple straight forward step by step guide on how to make a simple and cheap pot still.

Is this book for you? If your interest, like me, is about having a go for fun, finding that boutique flavor, or scent then yes this is a good starting point. However if your interest is maximising the amount of alcohol from your wash in a single distillation, then probably not, you want a reflux or fractioning still not a pot still.

OK so you are still reading, and want to try your hand at distillation or are looking for a step by step guide to making a really simple and cheap but effective pot still. To ensure I am not breaching any state, federal, or international laws, I advise if you decide to go ahead to produce alcohol or oils from your still, look up and read your country's federal and state laws on the legalities and tax requirements for operating a still. If owning a still is illegal where you are REMEMBER it can be used as, and called an "evaporative water purifier".

Although this book is a step by step guide to making a Pot Still, and not a how to distill book, there is some basic information that is handy to know to better understand the whys and how it works. More detailed information as I said earlier is available on the internet.

Distillation Basics

At sea level, alcohol boils at 78 °C (172 °F), while water boils at 100 °C (212 °F). During distillation, the vapour contains more alcohol than the liquid. When the vapours are condensed, the resulting liquid contains a higher concentration of alcohol.

To distill alcohol you start with a fermented wash.

The simplest wash consists of sugar, yeast and water. This is fermented in a container until all the sugar is consumed by the yeast, anywhere from 24 hours to 10 days depending on how the sugar is contained (refined or in fruit or as starch in grain) and the resulting wash is usually around 5 to 7% alcohol. Some of the specialty yeasts designed for wine and alcohol brewing can produce up to 14% in 24 to 48 hours.

When fermentation is complete you put the wash in the still and heat it. The vapour that boils off rises to the space at the top. The evaporation process increases the pressure inside the pot forcing the vapour into the swan neck and then into the condenser. As it cools, because alcohol boils at a lower temperature than water, the resulting liquid coming out of the condenser outlet contains a much higher concentration of alcohol than the initial wash.

Still Types

There are three different types of still, pot, reflux and fractioning stills.

A POT still collects and condenses the vapours given off by boiling the wash. In the pot still, the alcohol and water vapour combine with esters and flow from the still through the condensing coil. There they condense into the first distillation liquid, called "low wines". The low wines have a strength of about 25-35% alcohol by volume but plenty of flavour (essence) is retained. Passing the "Low wines" through the still a second time will produce the colourless spirit, collected at about 70% alcohol by volume. Colour is added through maturation in an oak aging barrel, and develops over time.

A REFLUX still does these multiple distillations in one single pass. Packing in a column between the condenser & the pot, and allows some of the vapour to condense and trickle back down through the packing. This "reflux" of liquid means only the purest vapour raises to the very top and increase the % purity. The taller the packed column, and the more reflux liquid, the purer the product will be. The advantage of doing this is that it will result in a clean ethanol (clear alcohol), with little flavour to it - ideal for mixing with flavours etc.

A FRACTIONATING column is a pure form of the reflux still. It will condense all or most of the vapour at the top of the packing, and return 90% of the vapour back down the column. The column will be quite tall - compared to the boiler, and packed with a material high in surface area, but which takes up little space (something like steel wool). It will result in an alcohol 95%+ pure (the theoretical limit without using a vacuum is 95.6%), with no other tastes or impurities in it.

Note that both reflux and fractionating stills can still be used to make whisky, rum etc, as they allow a very precise "cut" between the heads, middle, and tail runs.

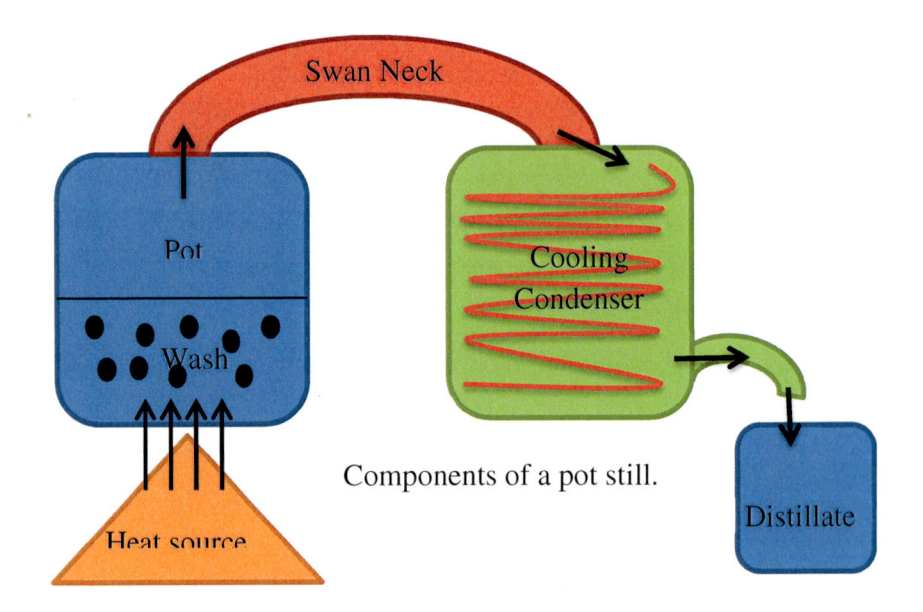

Components of a pot still.

Parts of a still

There are three main parts to a pot still, a sealable container (the Pot), a Condenser (Cooling Coil) and the pipe (the Swan Neck or Lyne Arm) linking the pot and condenser.

For the pot I am using a pressure cooker, and for the condenser coil and swan neck some ½ inch copper plumbers pipe.

Parts List

NOTE: These are the parts I have used because they were available cheap. If you want to try something else, do so. Also don't get too pedantic about the sizes, the important thing is they fit together and work. I used the parts to fit the copper pipe. Had I used 3/8 inch pipe instead of 1/2 inch, I would have used fittings to suit. This list and book are only a guide, not rules.

Parts Used

	Description	Qty
1	NAMCO 6 litre Pressure Cooker	1 ea
2	20 litre metal bucket	1 ea
3	15mm Female Compression Union	3 ea
4	15mm Male Compression Union	1 ea
5	15 mm Coupler female to female	1 ea
6	15mm threaded plug	1 ea
7	15mm FlangedBasin Nut	4 ea
8	15mm Rubber seals/ washers	4 ea
9	15mm threadedbasin pipe	150 mm
10	½ inch (13mm) copper pipe	4 m
11	6mm male to 15mm male nipple	1
12	15mm cistern tap Female to male	1
13	NAMCO seal set for pressure cooker	1

A NAMCO six litre (or a NAMCO 16 pint (9 litre)) pressure cooker is best, however any pressure cooker with only the pressure release bell and a single safety seal in the lid will work. NAMCO cookers are easy to find, cheap, and easy to get replacement seals for. If there are other openings they will need to be sealed. Threaded holes can be sealed with a bolt and rubber washer/seal. Non threaded holes with nut bolt and rubber washer.

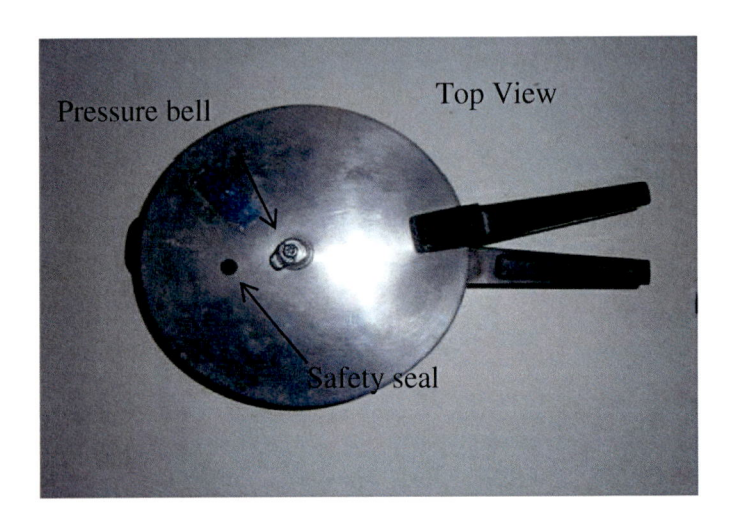

10

20 litre (4 or 5 gallon) metal bucket/ drum, the kind that paint or beef lard come in. This is to house the cooling coil.

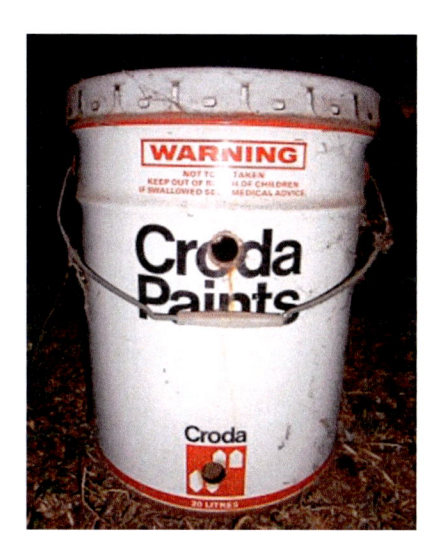

15mm Female Compression Union. (One of these is to join the swan neck to the pot the other two are for the inlet and outlet ends of condenser coil.)

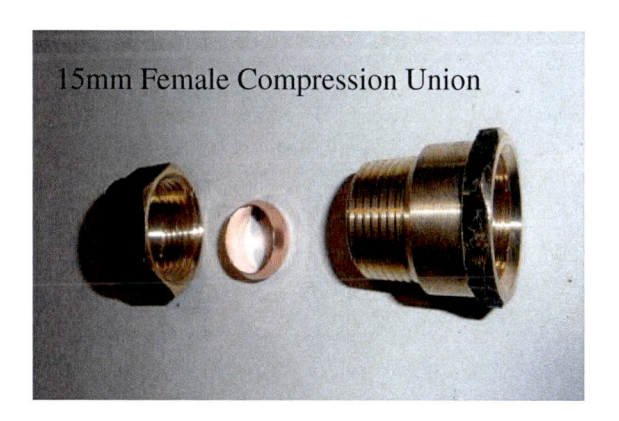

11

15mm Male Compression Union. (This with a 15mm female to female Coupler is for joining the swan neck to the Condenser.)

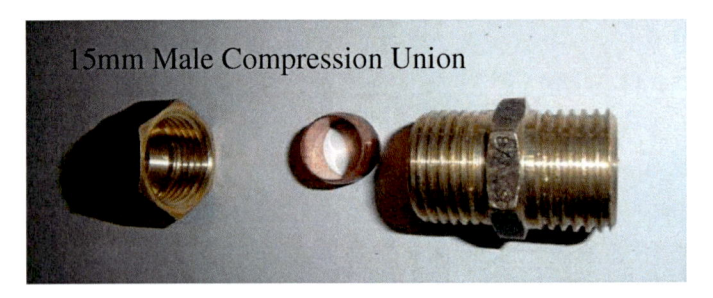

15mm Male Compression Union

Note: You could use a 15mm female, however when the still is not in use, I use a 15mm plug (See below) screwed into the 15 mm coupler attached to your condenser to stop the hornets making mud nests in the pipe. Trust me it can be a hell of a job to clean out once there.

Coupler

15mm female to female coupler.

See previous note

12

15mm threaded plug. Not crucial to the still but can be useful to stop hornet infestations.

Plug

15mm flanged basin nuts. These are used with the 4 rubber seals and the threaded basin pipe as the means of passing the condenser inlet and outlet through the bucket.

Flanged Basin Nut

15mm rubber washers/ seals

15mm rubber washers

15mm threaded brass basin pipe. You will need to cut this in half so you have two 75mm (approximatley) lengths.

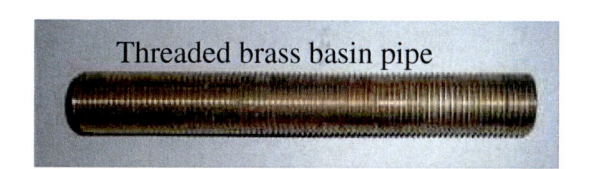

Threaded brass basin pipe

13

½ inch copper pipe. How long really depends on how big you make your condenser. You need approximatly 750mm for the swan neck and if you don't use a tap, 150 to 200 mm for the outlet

Copper Pipe

6mm male x 15mm male Nipple. The size of this will actually depend on the size of the thread on the bottom of the pressure bell stem. The NAMCO 6 litre cooker I am using has a 6mm threaded hole. Since I was only able to get a 6mm x 10mm nipple, I also bought a 10mm x 15mm bush.

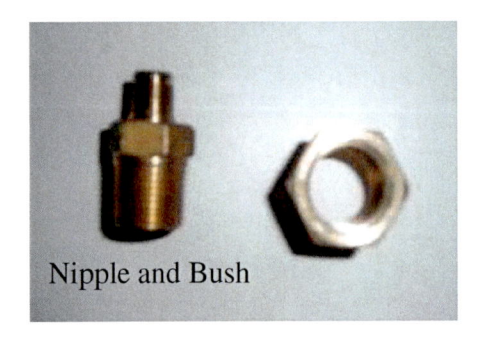

Nipple and Bush

14

15mm Cistern Tap. This is for the condenser outlet. You do not need this. A short length of pipe will do the same thing. This just makes it easier to change your distillate collector while still in operation.

WARNING: Tap must remain open while operating. Do not leave tap shut when operating the still. You could pressurise the system to dangerous levels. They made this mistake at Chernobyl, look what happened there.

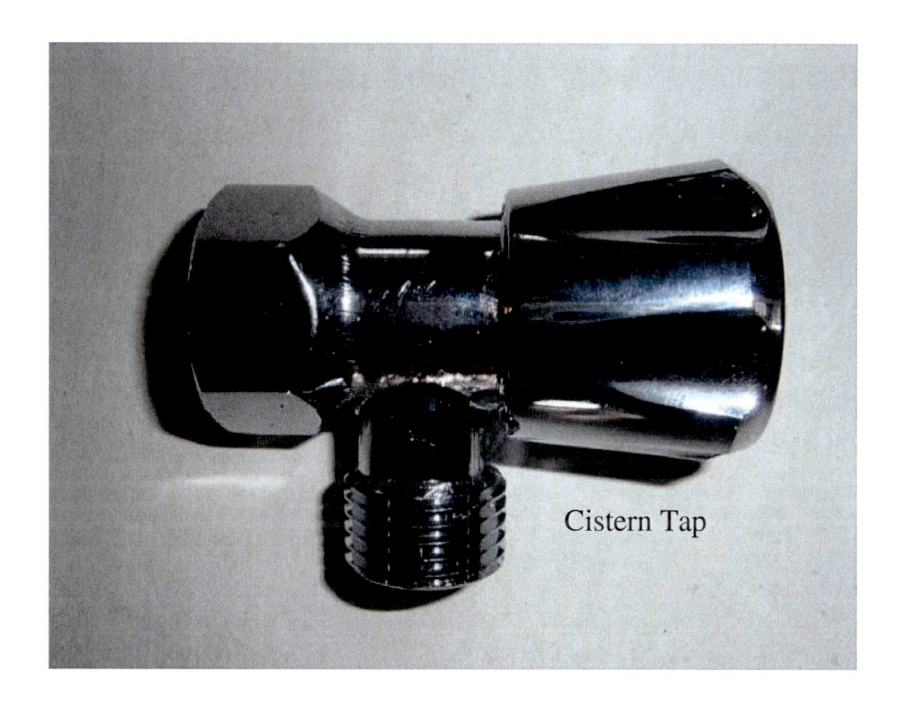

Cistern Tap

15

Getting Started

If you are an experienced handy man and have a good grasp of plumming problems then you can skip this bit and head straight to Step 1.

Hints and tips before starting.

When buying parts shop around. Speak to a plumber or builder. You get better prices from a plumbing supplier than from the handyman store.

Every join is a potential leak point. The less joins in the system the less potential leak points. Compression fittings are designed not to leak. (Read the bit on compression fittings.) All the non-compression threaded joins need to be tight. If they still leak, thread tape (or some other joint seal) can be used but ensure it can be used in heated water situations. To check for leaks once the unit is complete, set it up for use with only water in the pot, coat all joins with dishwashing detergent, and bring to the boil. Turn the tap off for about a minute and leaky joins should make bubbles in the detergent.

Compression fittings

Compression fittings are used in plumbing and electrical conduit systems to join two tubes or thin-walled pipes together. In instances where two pipes made of dissimilar materials are to be joined (most commonly PVC and copper), the fittings will also be made of one or more compatible materials appropriate for the connection. Compression fittings for attaching tubing (piping) commonly have ferrules (or *olives* in the UK) in them.

Compression fittings are also used extensively for hot and cold water faucets (taps) and toilet stop valves; compression fittings are well suited to this application, as these valves are usually located in confined spaces where copper pipe would be difficult to solder without creating a fire hazard.

Compression fittings are the industry standard for chemical, oil and gas, R&D, Bio-tech, and the semiconductor industry.

They are used due to their ability to provide leak-tight seals. These fittings can be remade.

How compression fittings work

In small sizes, the compression fitting is composed of an outer *compression nut* and an inner *compression ring* or ferrule that is typically made of brass or copper. Ferrules vary in shape and material but are most commonly in the shape of a ring with beveled edges. To work properly, the ferrule must be oriented correctly -- usually the ferrule is fitted such that the longest sloping face of the ferrule faces away from the nut.

When the nut is tightened, the ferrule is compressed between the nut and the receiving fitting; the ends of the ferrule are clamped around the pipe, and the middle of the ferrule bows away from the pipe, making the ferrule effectively thicker. The result is that the ferrule seals the space between the pipe, nut, and receiving fitting, thereby forming a tight joint.

Thread sealants such as joint compound (pipe dope or thread seal tape such as PTFE tape) are unnecessary on compression fitting threads, as it is not the thread that seals the joint but rather the compression of the ferrule between the nut and pipe. However, a small amount of plumber's grease or light oil applied to the threads will provide lubrication to help ensure a smooth, consistent tightening of the compression nut.

It is critical to avoid over-tightening the nut or else the integrity of the compression fitting will be compromised by the excessive force. If the nut is over tightened the ferrule will deform improperly causing the joint to fail. Indeed, over tightening is the most common cause of leaks in compression fittings. A good rule of thumb is to tighten the nut first by hand until it is too difficult to continue and then tighten the nut one half-turn more with the aid of a wrench; the actual amount varies with the size of the fitting, as a larger one requires less tightening. The fitting is then tested: if slight weeping is observed, the fitting is gradually tightened until the weeping stops.

The integrity of the compression fitting is determined by the ferrule, which is easily prone to damage. Thus care should be taken to when handling and tightening the fitting, although if the ferrule is damaged it is easily replaced.

Step 1.

If it's not already gone remove the pressure release bell.

Remove the pressure release bell

Step 1

The Pressure release bell will just lift off.

18

Step 2.

Unscrew the bell stem from the lid of the pressure cooker.

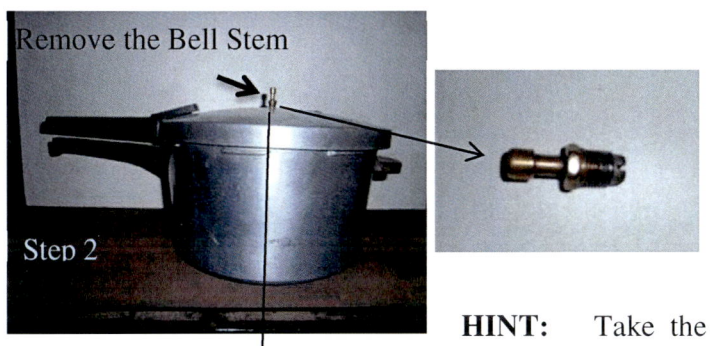

Remove the Bell Stem

Step 2

HINT: Take the bell stem with you when you go in to get your fittings to ensure you get the correct size with the correct thread.

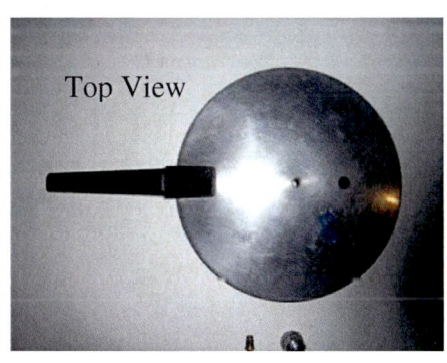

Top View

Step 3.

Screw a 15mm female compression union on to the 6 x 15 mm nipple.

Step 4.

Screw the 6mm x 15mm male to male nipple into the hole the bell stem was removed from.

Male Nipple and Compression Union

Step 4

This completes the "POT"

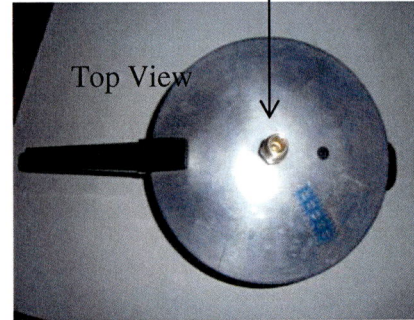

Top View

20

Step 5.

In the 20 litre metal bucket you need to cut two holes. Placement of these holes will be dictated by where you need them to be in relation to the heat source (which will be under the POT), and by the shape of your work space you are in.

For this project I have put the top inlet and bottom outlet on opposite sides. These can be place where ever you need them

See the examples below.

**NOTE: INLET IS AT THE TOP
OUTLET IS AT THE BOTTOM**

Example 1. Inlet and outlet on opposite sides.

21

Example 2. Inlet and outlet at right angles. With inlet to the left side.

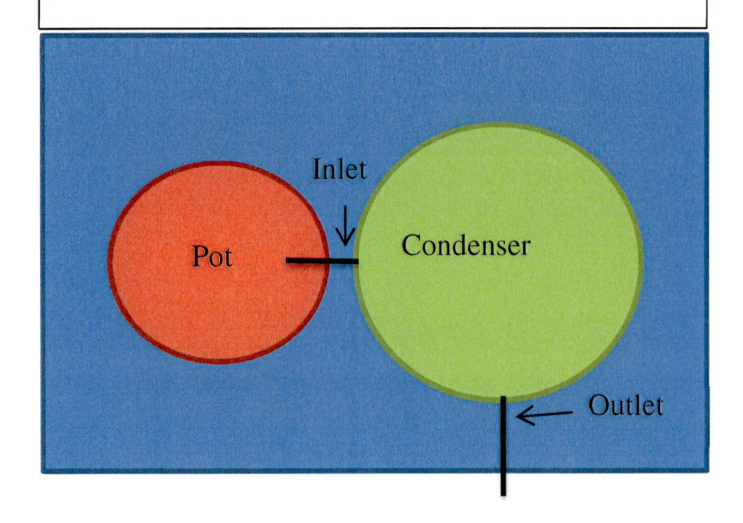

Pot — Inlet ↓ — Condenser

← Outlet

Example 3. Inlet and outlet at right angles. With inlet to the right side.

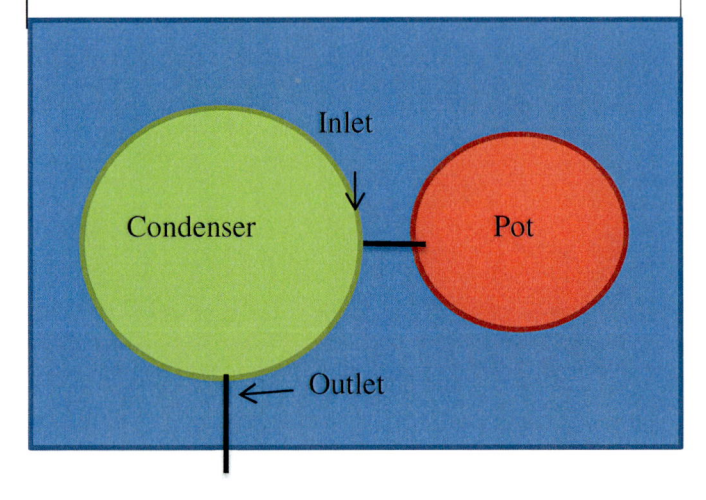

Condenser — Inlet ↓ — Pot

← Outlet

The holes in the bucket need to big enough to pass the threaded basin pipe through. These holes need to be made water tight. You could use a hole saw, or big drill bit, I used a 20 mm diameter plumbers hole punch. Make each hole about 50mm from the top and bottom edges respectively.

Step 6

Cut the threaded basin pipe in half and clean the cut ends with a file so the flanged nut will wind on smoothly.

You can see I was only precise to the nearest couple of centimeters. Near enough is close enough.

With two seals and two flanged basin nuts on each length of basin pipe, you are now set to attach these into the inlet and outlet holes.

Step 7.

Place the pipe through the inlet and outlet holes in the drum, with a seal on either side and secure with the flanged basin nuts. Make sure they are tight. They need to be water tight, otherwise water will leak into your work space.

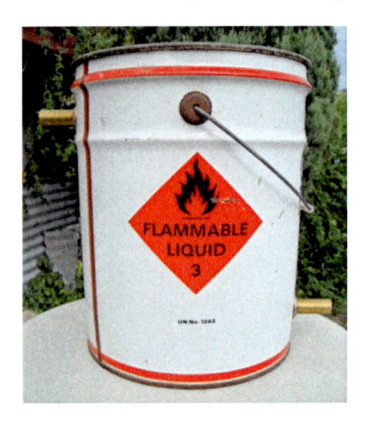

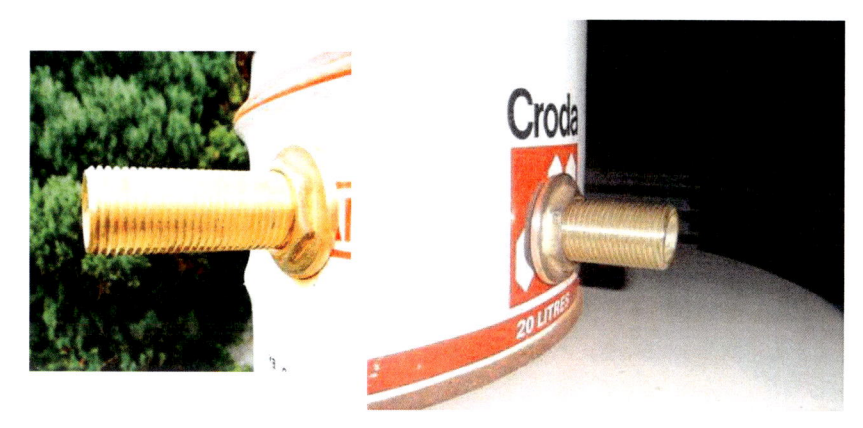

You could dispense with the seals, nuts and the basin pipe and fix the copper pipe through the bucket and solder or braze the holes to seal them, using a double sided pressure fitting to attach swan neck to the inlet of the condenser. However this requires a level of skill and equipment that many of us do not own. However it does reduce the number of joins, reducing the number of potential leak points. The pictures below are of such a condenser using 3/8 inch copper pipe and square metal washers to reinforce the bucket.

Step 8.

Next attach the cistern tap to the outside of the outlet.

You do not need a tap here. A short length of copper pipe attached with a compression union will work just as well.

You can shape it to suit your needs.

Step 9.

Now attach the 15mm coupler to the 15 mm male compression union and attach these to the outside of the inlet.

Step 10.

Next attach a 15mm female compression union to both the inside inlet and inside outlet of the basin pipe.

Step 11.

From the coil of copper pipe cut a length for the swan neck approximately 750mm long (and if you don't use a Tap a second length approximately 150 mm long for the distillate outlet as shown in step 8.)

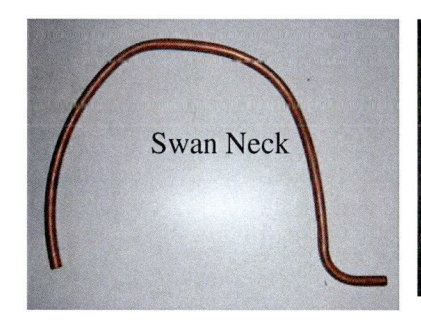

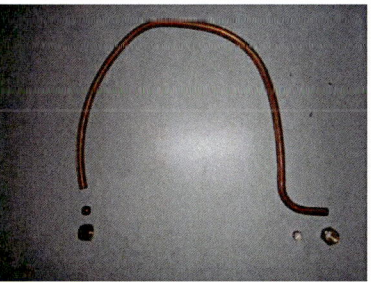

And fit the nuts and olives. If you are not familiar, with the use of compression fittings make sure you read about how to use them in pages 16 and 17.

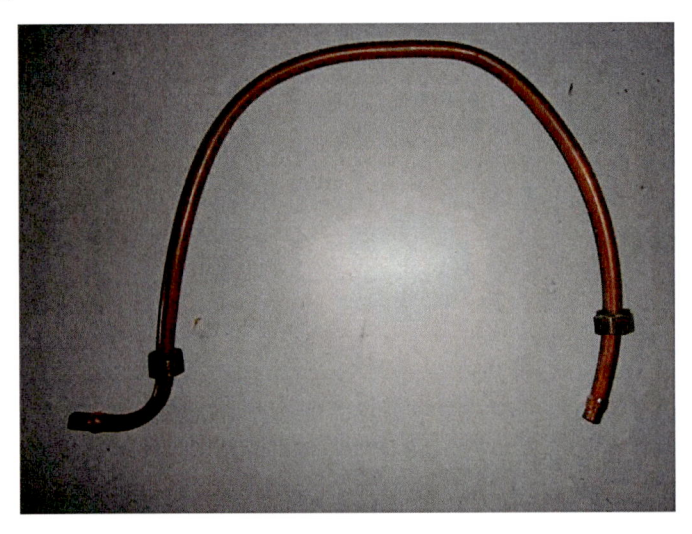

Step 12.

With the remaining copper pipe make a tight coil with the coils approximately 175 to 250 mm in diameter for the condenser coil. The important thing is that it fits inside the 20 litre drum.

Condenser Coil

Inlet and outlet on oposite sides.

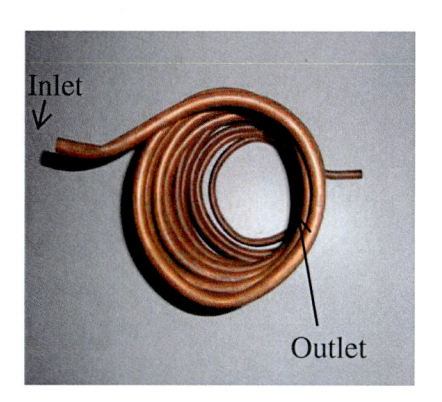

Hint: Be careful not to kink the pipe. The best way is to find something the size you want and wind the pipe around it. A piece of 8 inch poly pipe would work well. Whatever you use make sure you can slide the coil off and not have to unwind it.

Step 13.

Check the condenser coil fits in the bucket and the inlet and outlet line up with their respective attachment points and fit into place without too much horizontal or vertical tension. However if you find you don't have them lined up correctly you can work the coils bigger or smaller to line them up.

Make any adjustments (including shortening the inlet and outlet if necessary). A small block of wood or piece of paver can be put on the bottom of the bucket to rest the coil on and take its weight.

Step 14.

Once the coil sits correctly take it out and attach the nuts and olives.

Once the nuts and olives are in place re fit the coil into the bucket and tighten the nuts. Again if you are not familiar, with the use of compression fittings make sure you read about how to use them in pages 16 and 17.

31

This completes the condenser.

Step 15.

The final step is to fit the swan neck between the pot and condenser. Before you do this attach the pot end to the Pot and correctly tighten the compression nut. This will seat the olive so it won't slide off.

Next detach the pot and attach the swan neck to the inlet of the condenser and again correctly tighten the compression nut.

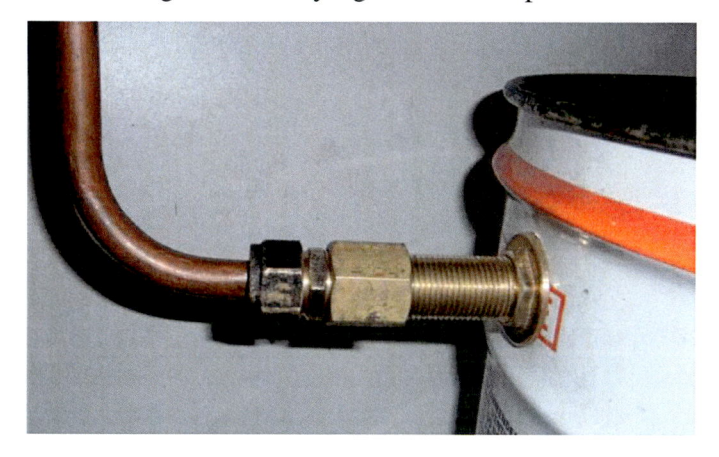

Detach the swan neck from the condenser. Take the three still components to where you intend to operate the still. Place the Pot on the proposed location of heat source and the condenser where it is proposed to sit. This is so you can correctly shape the swan neck. If the pot and still are to sit at the same level, then any bench top will do. You could also use small pieces of timber to build up the height difference between heat source and bench surface.

And that completes the POT STILL.

Saftey Tips.

Warning …. Be very careful when using the still. This thing gets HOT, there is steam trapped in the pot. Avoid taking the lid off the pot while it is still hot to touch. If you must, keep your body parts away from the top, to avoid potential steam burns. Wear gloves, eye protection and other heat protective clothing when assembling or disassembling when hot.

DO NOT leave the TAP OFF when using as you will potentially create over pressure in the system, this could have explosive results.

BE WARNED Alcohol is a poison. There is nothing heroic about consuming vast quantities of concentrated alcohol. Only potential death. It is a bit like arsnic, in small doses there are medicinal benefits, however the larger the dose the higher the risk of permanent damage or death.

Alcohol when concentrated is also highly flammable keep away from naked flames and keep naked flames away from it.

ENSURE WORK SPACE IS WELL VENTILATED. Concentrated vapour is Highly Explosive.

Made in the USA
San Bernardino, CA
19 June 2016